SURVIVAL OF A SPECIES:
THE ELEPHANT SEAL

SURVIVAL OF A SPECIES: THE ELEPHANT SEAL

BY JAMES T. CROW

PHOTOGRAPHS BY GORDON E. CHITTENDEN

WARD RITCHIE PRESS

The author wishes to acknowledge
the invaluable assistance of Daniel Odell, B.S., M.A., Ph.D.,
University of California at Los Angeles.

Copyright © 1971 by James T. Crow and Gordon E. Chittenden
Library of Congress Catalog Card Number 78-173233
ISBN 0378-60323-X
Printed in the United States of America
Design by Joseph Simon

CONTENTS

INTRODUCTION

Every living thing is the highly specialized result of the particular place it occupies in the universe. The leaves of the cactus plant are soft and thick for the storage of the moisture necessary for its survival. The fish has gills that enable it to take oxygen from the water in which it lives. The bat has its own form of radar to allow it to fly through absolute darkness in pursuit of its food. Each plant, each insect, each animal that exists today is the product of thousands of years of development during which it has become uniquely adapted to its environment.

One of the most interesting examples of this adaptation for survival is the seal. The seal is a mammal and must breathe air in order to live. Yet it must also be able to stay underwater for long periods of time as it searches for food. It is also a warm-blooded animal. So it must be able to stay warm even when it is in very cold water for months on end. Its young is also born alive, not hatched from an egg, as are most creatures of the sea. So it must be nursed by its mother until it is sufficiently strong to secure its own food.

It is difficult to imagine that any mammal would be able to adapt to such hostile conditions as living in the sea. Yet the seal has accomplished this and in addition, making it unique even among marine mammals, it is also able to stay on land several months on end with no ill effects. A most remarkable animal.

In this book we will examine one kind of seal and discuss the intricate and fascinating adaptations it has made in order to survive in its environment. Our subject is the elephant seal, the largest of them all.

Chapter 1
LIFE AMONG THE ELEPHANT SEALS

What are they like, these elephant seals? Where do they live? If you were to visit one of the places where they live, what would you find? Let us describe a trip we made to the San Benito Islands off the west coast of the Baja California peninsula in Mexico.

These islands are about 325 miles south of San Diego, California. On our 85-foot-long sports fishing boat it took about 20 hours for us to get there. We anchored off shore and in small outboard motor boats we landed in a small cove.

The island looked like the top of a mountain sticking up out of the ocean. The land climbed abruptly from the water to make tall, rocky cliffs and on the shore line there were coves and inlets. It was in these that we would find the elephant seals.

Rugged coastline typical of the San Benitos. In spring, hundreds of elephant seals are found in the secluded coves.

After walking through a small fishing village we climbed up a narrow path above the cliffs. After a half mile or so, those with the sharpest ears began to hear the elephant seals. Far in the distance there was a faint, curious noise that sounded like "Toink . . . toink . . . toink . . ." The leader of our group, Dr. William Burns of the San Diego Museum of Natural History, told us this was the battle-cry of the elephant seal bull.

We hurried on and after rounding a shoulder of the mountain we worked our way down to the edge of the cliffs. Below us on a small sandy beach were the elephant seals. The nearest group was made up of one bull, a dozen cows and three or four pups. The cows saw us on the cliff and watched us with their large, dark eyes. One, lying with her chin on the back of a neighbor, absently scooped up sand with her flippers and tossed it onto her back.

The cows were brown, the hair on their stomachs lighter than on their backs. The bull was a darker shade and much larger. Stretched out on the sand, we estimated him to be about 14 feet

In a small cove we found a small harem of ten cows and a couple of small pups watched over by one big bull.

The adult male elephant seal has a broad, calloused chest and his body is marked with many scars.

long. The cows were smaller, perhaps eight feet. The pups were about three feet long and their fur was dark gray, almost black.

A little further away on a larger beach was a bigger group of perhaps a hundred. These were much noisier and we could hear a confused chorus of snorts, sneezes, coughs and growls. In the calm surf a few feet offshore, a large bull reared up. With his chest thrust out and his head back, his big snout hung down into his mouth. "Toink . . . toink . . . toink . . ." The noise was like a series of grunts but with a sharper, more resonant tone.

Another bull, this one a few feet from the water, rose up into the same position and replied, "Toink . . . toink . . . toink . . ." Then he splashed into the surf, vaulting along on his short front flippers, the rest of his body working along behind like a caterpillar.

The two bulls faced each other in the water, both standing high on their flippers, heads weaving back and forth. Then they smacked together, hard. The first bull, the one that had issued the

11

Fights between the bulls sometimes take place in the shallow water near the beach where the harem is gathered.

12

original challenge, turned and splashed away, heading for deeper water and swam out into the cove. The other bull watched him for a moment, then returned to shore.

We had to go a couple hundred yards further inland before we found a path that led down to the beach. Near the end of the path beside a large rock was a small elephant seal, looking up at us. His eyes were big and dark, the fur on his cheeks streaked with tears as if he were crying. He was about four feet long and very fat, so fat that he had several double chins.

As we watched him, he yawned and scratched his neck, a gesture that was so human that we laughed. On the ends of his short front flippers there were black fingernails shaped much like our own. The flipper had five "fingers" and his black palm made him look like he was wearing fine black gloves.

Going past him onto the beach we saw several more of the small elephant seals in groups of two and three. Some watched us as we walked among them but they gave no sign they were

The front flippers, which have five "fingers," are used almost like hands. Here one is scratching his head.

13

Color of the coat changes with age. Young pups are very dark,
weaned pups are tan and adults a dark brown.

afraid of us. Others did not even bother to wake up. These were recently weaned pups that had been born on this beach this year. They had already shed their dark gray puppy fur and the coarse hair on their bodies varied from a soft tan to a light brown.

The main part of the group was near the water and as we got closer, we noticed that the small, black pups were making more than their share of the racket. We watched one of the noisiest of the pups for some time. He was never quiet, the inside of his mouth a bright pink as he carried on. He acted fussy. Not hungry, not mad, not hurt, just *fussy* and wanting everyone to know it, the way a human baby will sometimes do.

We stood 15 or 20 feet from the large group and they paid no attention to us at all. They lay close together, some half on top of another. Many of them had sand on their backs and at almost any time we could see one of them flipping sand up onto its back.

Near the center of the jumble of cows was a very large bull. He was the one we had seen drive the other bull away when we

14

were watching from the cliffs. It was obvious that he was the boss of this group. We called him the beachmaster. As we watched, he propped himself up on his front flippers, put his head back and issued a challenge. "Toink . . . toink . . . toink . . ."

Then he waited. On the other side of the harem, another bull rose up. But after looking over to see who had made the challenge, he lay right back down again and remained silent.

The beachmaster looked around, ready to fight. But when his invitation to battle went unanswered, he settled down among the cows again.

The bulls around the edge of the harem were far more active. One we soon began to recognize we called the "devout coward." He issued many challenges, as if he were ready to fight every bull in the vicinity. But when another bull responded, he quickly lay down again, not interested in fighting at all.

Once, not having noticed another bull a few feet away, he got caught. The other bull sprang up, rushing toward him, scram-

Bulls pay no attention to the pups. Here a huge bull is running over a pup. This one wasn't seriously hurt.

Bulls fight for dominance in the harem. Here the "beachmaster" (right) prepares to put a challenger in his place.

bling over a couple of cows that were in his path and ran right over a squawling black pup.

Our devout coward tried to get away but it was too late and he got a couple hard blows from the head of his attacker before he could escape. He headed for the water, splashing into the surf and swimming out into the cove.

The pup that had been run over by the bull lay motionless, its fur covered with sand. We knew that many pups were killed this way and we feared the same fate had befallen this one. The cow we had seen nursing him earlier was only a few feet away but she paid no attention to him at all.

After a few minutes the pup opened its mouth. A little later it began to move and soon it was fussing again, as noisily as ever. Apparently it had escaped serious injury this time.

In a period of a couple hours the beachmaster only had to fight one other bull. We watched from a few feet away, close enough to see the callouses on his huge chest and how the throat

Bull elephant seals go through a ritual challenge before they rush toward each other and begin their battle.

and snout pulsed in rhythm with the "toink . . . toink . . . toink . . ." Then the two bulls rushed each other, mindless of the cows and pups in between.

They came together with a great thump, mouths open, heads slashing down, their big, sharp teeth aimed at the throat of the other. After three or four blows, the challenger tried to rush past the beachmaster to make his escape. The beachmaster bit him once in the shoulder, once in the middle of the back, then once more near the rear flippers before he could get away.

Later we walked on around the island, looking at other groups in the coves and inlets. In one tiny inlet we saw one large bull with two old cows. These three lay in a peaceful heap, sleeping, sand covering their backs. They seemed like old folks that had given up the hustle and bustle of harem life and were enjoying their retirement.

In another larger cove we found a bigger group and here there was the same restlessness as in the first. The bulls challenged and fought. The cows bickered among themselves, biting at each other's mouths rather than slapping hard with their heads like the bulls. Back away from the main group a young bull was annoying an immature cow. He was attempting to mate with her and being noisly rejected. A typical scene in an elephant seal harem during breeding time.

Altogether there were perhaps a thousand elephant seals on the island that day. We watched them until late afternoon and were sorry when we had to go back to the boats. As we trudged along the path around the shoulder of the mountain, the noise of the big harem faded slowly. The last sound we could distinguish was another challenge being issued, "Toink . . . toink . . . toink . . . toink . . ." and we knew that life was going on among the elephant seals just as it had for thousands of years.

Adult male elephant seal. Typically, no part of the ear is visible from outside and the front flippers are short.

19

Chapter 2
THE ORDER OF THE "FEATHERFOOT"

What strange animals elephant seals are. So different from most of the animals with which we are familiar. So odd looking compared to other mammals. Where did such curious animals come from? How did they develop? Why are they like they are?

To understand them, it is necessary to know a little about their place in the world of animals.

In the zoologist's way of classifying animals, there are three "orders," or types, of marine mammals. That is, mammals that live in the water. The first order is called the *Cetacea* and this includes the whale, porpoise and dolphin. Second is the *Sirenia* consisting of the sea cow, manatee and dugong. And the third is the *Pinnipedia*, which is made up of the seal, sea lion and walrus.

A sea lion can be readily distinguished from one of the true seals by the small ears on the sides of the head.

Harbor seal. Like all seals, it has no exterior parts to the ear and the front flippers are small.

The seal swims with wagging thrusts of its rear while front flippers are used only for balance and turning.

The first two of these orders must spend their entire lives in the water. But members of the third order (seals, sea lions and walruses) live for extended periods of time on dry land.

The literal translation of the Latin name, *Pinniped,* is "feather foot." This refers to the flipper. It is a good description because the flipper is the Pinniped's equivalent of the ordinary land-animal's foot and because it is, when stretched out, like a fan or a feather in appearance.

The three members of the order of the featherfoot are slightly different from each other. You can identify a seal (its zoological name is *Phocidae*) by the fact that it does not have ears that can be seen on the outside of the head. A sea lion (*Otariidae*) looks similar at first glance but it has fleshy little ear shells. The third Pinniped, the walrus (*Obodendae*), has a blunt nose, goggly eyes and a pair of large tusks that make certain it will not be mistaken for either of the other two.

There are also other ways to tell a seal from a sea lion. They

Long tusks of the walrus make certain that it will not be mistaken for either a seal or a sea lion.

swim differently, for example. A seal swims by shoving itself through the water with powerful side-to-side strokes of the tail flippers. But the sea lion swims by propelling itself through the water with strong, sculling motions of its long front flippers.

They also walk in different ways when they are on land. A sea lion can turn its rear flippers forward. This enables it to lift its entire body off the ground and a sea lion can move along at a rapid pace. A seal cannot do this so it scoots along on its belly, using the short front flippers almost like crutches and the rest of the body is hunched along behind.

Altogether there are 18 different species of seal and they are found in three main geographical areas of the world. The largest number are found in the arctic and antarctic but some congregate in the Tropic of Cancer and there is one species that lives in the Hawaiian islands.

The smallest seal is the Baikal seeal (*Pusa sibirica*), which is about four feet long and weighs about 150 pounds. The largest is

The sea lion swims by pulling itself through the water with sculling motions of its long front flippers.

*On land, the sea lion turns its rear flippers forward and is
thereby able to lift its body off the ground.*

*A seal cannot turn its rear flippers forward, so it uses its short
front flippers to hunch itself along.*

the elephant seal and the adult male sometimes is as long as 22 feet and weighs as much as 6000 to 8000 pounds. This is as long and as heavy as a very large automobile!

There are two closely related species of elephant seal. The southern variety (*Mirounga leonina*) is found mostly in the antarctic and sub-antarctic while the northern type (*Mirounga angustirostris*) lives half a world away on remote islands off the coast of southern California and northern Mexico. These two are very similar. Both engage in sandflipping, for instance, and they are the only species of seals that do this. They are very alike in appearance, except that the northern bull has a much larger snout. The southern variety is slightly larger in overall size. At one time there was undoubtedly only one type of elephant seal. Then, in some unexplained way, the group became divided with one going to live in the southern hemisphere, the other in the northern. Because of differences in the environments in which they lived, the two species became slightly different; one developed a longer

One of the peculiar habits of the elephant seal is "sand flipping." They are the only seals that do this.

The northern elephant seal is huge and when propped up on its front flippers is almost as tall as a man.

The largest adult male elephant seals may be as long and as heavy as a very large automobile.

snout, the other became larger. It is not understood why these things happened but it is an excellent example of the way some animals are slightly different when they live in different surroundings in a different part of the world.

The southern elephant seal lives in what is usually a cold climate. The largest number are found on South Georgia Island, a colony of the British Antarctic Territory about a thousand miles east of the tip of South America. Altogether, it is estimated that there are 600,000 to 700,000 southern elephant seals.

The northern elephant seal lives in a much more temperate climate. The largest congregation is on Guadalupe Island, which is about 220 miles west of Ensenada, Baja California, Mexico. There are perhaps as many as 10,000 of them here during the breeding season. Sizable groups are also found on other remote islands in the same general vicinity.

In earlier times before elephant seals were hunted for their oil, they were much more widely distributed than at present. In the early 1800s, for example, northern elephant seals were commonly found as far north as Point Reyes near San Francisco, California, and as far south as Cabo San Lazaro, more than three hundred miles south of Ensenada. There are now about 15,000-20,000 northern elephant seals and it is believed that their numbers are increasing.

Chapter 3
THE ORIGINS OF THE SEAL

As you know, scientific investigation indicates that all forms of life on earth had their origins millions of years ago in the warm waters of the oceans. As eons passed, some of these sea animals moved onto land and became adapted to living on shore.

Those animals that were to develop into mammals became warm-blooded, they learned to breathe air and their young were born alive to be nursed by their mothers. The animals that remained in the sea, the fish, did not do this.

As thousands and thousands of years passed many of the mammals became completely adapted to life on land. This change in their environment was so complete that some animals, like man, became totally unsuited to a life in water. If they were to go into

An otter swims much like a seal; that is, by pushing itself through the water with wagging thrusts of its tail.

The seal's flippers have five "fingers" and are equipped with fingernails much like our own.

The seal, like the otter, holds its front flippers close to its body when it is swimming.

the water, they had to learn to swim and none of their normal life functions, such as breathing or eating or sleeping, could be carried on there.

Yet not all mammals remained on the land. A few of them, even though they had become true warm-blooded mammals, returned to live in the sea again. It is probably true that these had remained near the water rather than moving in-shore to a completely dry-land eixstence. But the fact remains that they had their origins in the sea, came to land and evolved into air-breathing mammals, and then returned to live in the sea again. These are what we now know as the marine mammals.

One of the mammals that returned to live in the sea was the ancestor of the seal. That the seal's ancestor was at one time adapted to living on land and is related to other land mammals can be deduced from several of the seal's physical characteristics. The seal's flippers, for instance, were at one time much more like the legs and feet of today's land mammals. It is no coincidence

The featherfoot's rear flippers are fan-like and are similar to the swim fins used by human swimmers.

that the seal's front flippers contain all the same bones that are found in the human arm and hand. Although these are of different proportions than in man, the seal has an elbow, a wrist, and not only are there five "fingers" in a seal's fin, the flipper is also complete with fingernails.

In the ages since the seal's ancestor returned to the sea, his "land" legs slowly changed to be better suited to life in the water. The bones of the arm became shorter and the bones of the "fingers" extended to their present length. With a covering of skin that stretched between the fingers, a much more efficient swimming device was created. The "featherfoot" is a perfect design for its purpose. Man's imitation of it in swim fins demonstrates that no better model could be found.

There are two theories as to the origins of the Pinnipeds. One is that they all descended from an animal that was similar to that which we now know as the otter. The other idea is that there were two different ancestors, the seal having evolved from the otter

The sea lion, though obviously related to the seal, swims by pulling itself through the water with its front flippers.

One idea about the origin of seals is that they descended from the same primeval ancestor as the otter.

while the sea lion and walrus descended from a primeval dog or bear.

While this argument may never be completely resolved, there are good reasons for acceptance of the two-ancestor theory. For example, the different ways in which the seal and sea lion swim suggests that the two came from basically different parentage. The sea otter and the seal have many characteristics in common. They swim in the same way, forcing themselves through the water with powerful wagging thrusts of their rear ends. On the other hand, the sea lion swims by pulling itself along with its front flippers, much like a dog or a bear.

It is impossible to say why the seal's ancestor returned to the sea to develop into a marine mammal. Maybe land-dwelling enemies made it impossible for them to survive on land. Perhaps they were unable to find sufficient food on land because of changes in the earth's climate. Whatever the reason, its adaptation to the water did not result in its becoming a completely water-dependent

A dog paddles through the water using its front feet in a manner that is more like a sea lion than a seal.

marine mammal like the whale which, even though it is an air-breathing animal, cannot survive out of water for more than a few hours. Even today the seal has certain vital activities that it must carry out on land.

The main reason for the seal's coming onto land has to do with reproduction. Although some species of seals do breed in the water, most do this on land. Furthermore, seal pups are born and the entire nursing period takes place on land. Seals also come out of the water when they molt; that is, when they lose their old coat of fur and grow another. The seal is also sufficiently at home on land that it may haul itself out of the water after feeding to simply lie on the beach to rest and sleep.

So the animal we now know as the seal is a remarkable one. For its origins in the sea millions of years ago, it first emigrated to land to become a mammal, then returned to the water again and re-adapted itself to life in that hostile environment. The seal is not alone in having been able to make almost unbelievable changes in its body in order to survive. But because the seal lives in two worlds, dependent both upon land and water for its survival, it is of greater interest than most animals who inhabit only one of these environments.

Chapter 4
SPECIALIZED FOR SURVIVAL

Physically, the seal is wonderfully well suited to its environment. Its physical characteristics add up to a miracle of efficiency for the life it lives.

First of all, a seal is the right shape for living in the water. In general, it is shaped like a drop of water as it falls through the air. This is the most streamlined shape possible. The seal's body is very smooth which makes it easier to move through the water. And the seal is extremely limber, which enables it to change direction very quickly in pursuit of its food.

It is not as well suited to life on land. There the seal is comparatively slow and awkward. But it is able to move itself about well enough to perform those acts that are necessary for its sur-

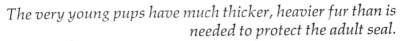

The very young pups have much thicker, heavier fur than is needed to protect the adult seal.

The layer of fat under the skin is important for warmth and streamlining in the water and as an energy source on land.

vival. In the water, pushed along by its powerful tail flippers, it can swim as fast as 15 to 18 miles an hour. On land, it can put on a brief burst of speed, perhaps up to about five miles an hour. But its flippers are not designed for movement on land (not like a dog's legs, for instance) and such actions take a tremendous amount of effort by the seal.

All seals have fur and this is important in helping to insulate them from the heat and cold when they are out of the water. (When they are wet, the fur is of no value as insulation as the water immediately penetrates to the skin.) A baby seal has thicker fur than an adult, the protective covering being more important to the not-yet-strong infant. Because this insulation becomes less important as the seal matures, the older the animal, the less thick its fur will be. Because it is not needed, not all seals are completely covered with fur when they are fully grown, one of the examples being the hard, calloused skin on the chest of the male elephant seal. So even the fur of the seal changes depending on the need the animal has for its protection.

Instead of fur, the elephant seal bull has a thick protective covering of calloused skin on his chest.

Under the skin of the seal there is a layer of fat. On the elephant seal this may be as much as six inches thick. Fat is excellent insulating material and is important because it enables the seal to retain its body heat even when it is in very cold water for long periods of time. In addition, the fat rounds out the seal's figure, making it more efficiently streamlined.

The fat carried on a seal's body is also important when it comes to shore for an extended stay. Since seals do not feed when they are on land, their bodies draw on this store of fat for the energy that is required during this time.

Because a seal's body is proportionately longer than that of a land mammal, it has a long backbone. Seals have 40 to 42 vertebrae, depending on the species, which is seven to nine more than a human being has at birth. The design of the vertebrae is such that the backbone is considerably more flexible than in most mammals and this gives the seal the ability to twist and turn very quickly in the water.

The backbone of the seal is extremely flexible; this enables it to maneuver very efficiently underwater.

Excellent eyesight, acute hearing, sensitive whiskers and possibly echo-location make the seal an efficient hunter.

The reproductive system of the elephant seal is like that of other mammals but here too there have been special adaptations that make the seal better suited to its environment. The genital organs of both the male and female seal are located underneath the skin in the blubber, which aids in streamlining the body.

The ribs of the seal lie more nearly parallel to the spine than do the ribs of a human being. This assists in allowing the lungs to be fully compressed when the seal dives. This is important because it enables the seal's body to achieve what is called "neutral buoyancy." This means that the body neither sinks nor floats and is therefore much easier to maneuver underwater. A man's body, because he cannot force all the air from his lungs, has "positive buoyancy." Consequently, a diver must add weights to his diving suit to achieve the neutral buoyancy of the seal.

The mouth of the seal is large and contains 30 to 40 teeth, depending on the species. At the front of the mouth are chisel-shaped incisors much like our own. These are the right design for cutting into the food that is to be eaten. The most prominent teeth are pointed, like dog's teeth, and these are used for tearing the food into chunks. Seals do not have well developed molars, as human beings do, since they tear off pieces of food and swallow them without chewing. To help hold the food more securely, the teeth are pointed slightly toward the rear of the mouth.

Underwater the seal is able to swallow its food without drawing water into its lungs. This is made possible by a valve that closes off the breathing passages from the gullet when the seal dives.

Little is known about the digestive process of the seal except that it takes place very rapidly. This too has its logic as this makes is possible for the seal to eat great amounts of food in a short period of time and thereby build up its reserves of fat for those intervals when it lives ashore.

The eyes of the seal are comparatively large and are designed in such a way as to give them better vision underwater than out of

*Elephant seals are extremely supple as shown by this bull that
has risen completely off his front flippers.*

water. The iris of the eye is transparent, which permits the maximum amount of light to enter, helping them see better in dim light. The location of the eyes is also important. These are near the sides of the head which gives them a better view of the things around them. If their eyes were in front, as they are in human beings, they would have to move their heads a greater distance when they were searching for food. Such a movement of the head would lessen the efficiency of their streamlining when swimming.

It is possible, however, that the seal does not depend entirely on its eyes in locating food. Blind seals have been studied and from their overall good physical condition it is apparent that they have been able to find sufficient food even without sight.

Underwater they make sounds that are described by scientists as "clicks." These sounds, combined with their extremely good hearing, are probably the seals' form of sonar that helps them find the fish, squid and other small sea animals that make up their diet even when they are deep in the ocean's black depths, and they cannot see.

Also, the seal's whiskers, which are very sensitive, may be important in locating their food.

If you recall our earlier description, you will remember that seals do not have any external parts of the ear. Instead, there is only a small hole on each side of the head. This does not mean the seal does not hear well, however. Indeed, the seal has very good hearing and underwater, where sound is more efficiently transmitted than in the air, the seal's hearing is remarkably acute.

The sense of smell is well developed in the seal. It is by this acute sense of smell, for instance, that the mother elephant seal is able to identify her pup. The sense of smell is not important to the seal when it is underwater. In fact, the nostrils automatically close to keep water out of the breathing passages when the seal dives. Although it has not been proven, it is speculated that the seal and other marine mammals have a highly developed sense of taste that allows them to detect the presence of food in the vicinity even before they are able to detect it with their sonar or see it

Because it is excellently suited to life in the water, a seal can live in the ocean for months at a time.

with their eyes. If this is true, then they must have the most sensitive taste buds of any animal in the world.

One of the most remarkable physical characteristics of the seal is that it is apparently not sensitive to pain in any degree comparable to that felt by all land-dwelling mammals. It is difficult to imagine but there are many indications that it is true. During the battles fought during breeding season, bull elephant seals bite each other severely and while they may grunt and roar with rage, they never make a sound that can be associated with pain. When the bull bites the cow as part of the mating ritual, the cow gives no sign that this hurts, neither crying out nor attempting to soothe the injured flesh.

Because of this lack of nerve response that we call pain, the elephant seal, before it was protected, was known among seal hunters as being "hard to kill." An elephant seal, though inflicted with wounds that would have caused almost any other mammal to be frantic with pain, would give no indication that it was suffering before it finally died.

45

This immunity from pain can also be observed in baby seals. The pups in an elephont seal harem receive very harsh treatment and while they are often noisy and fretful, even being run over by a charging bull doesn't cause a whimper that could be said to result from the effect of the injury. Even more dramatic is the fact that baby fur seals, before regulations were enforced to forbid it, were skinned alive by the seal hunters in order not to damage the pelts. Yet the baby seal did not react in any way that suggested it was experiencing pain in any degree appropriate to what was being done to it.

For an animal that lived on land, a similar lack of pain response to a flesh injury would create serious problems. The probability of infection resulting from dirt that would get into the wound is an excellent reason for the warning system of pain that notifies land animals of danger to their bodies. But without this pain response, the seal's life is made easier since damage to its flesh creates no discomfort. A bite from another seal or a cut inflicted by a sharp rock in the surf can simply be ignored. And because the seal spends most of its time in salt water, the wound is kept clean and therefore heals with a minimum risk of infection.

The seal is not alone in having this immunity to pain. Fish do not experience pain as we know it, nor do other ocean dwelling animals. So the seal, even though it is a mammal and would therefore be expected to experience pain, has adopted a characteristic of the true sea animal. This is another of the remarkable adaptations an animal's body can make to suit it for life in a hostile environment.

Because they must breathe free air in order to live, seals have made many remarkable adaptations to their environment.

Chapter 5

ADAPTATION:
THE KEY TO SURVIVAL

Two of the most interesting adaptations made by the mammals that live in the sea result from their being air-breathing, warm-blooded animals. For the fish, these are no problem. A fish doesn't breathe air, its gills extract oxygen from the water. A mammal can't do this; it must breathe free air. Also, a fish is cold-blooded; that is, its body is the same temperature as the water that surrounds it and can vary widely without harming the fish. But not a mammal. A mammal's vital organs must be kept at an almost constant temperature. For a human being this is 98.6 degrees. If it is only a degree or two more than this, we have a "fever." A degree

Returning to the surface after a long dive, the seal "pants" to catch its breath and restore its oxygen balance.

An elephant seal can stay underwater for at least 20 minutes without having to return to the surface to breathe.

As well as being specialized to spend much of their lives in the cold ocean, they are also able to live on land.

or two less causes a "chill." The adaptations that the seal's body has made to compensate for its being an air-breathing, warm-blooded mammal that lives in the sea are the keys to the seal's survival.

BREATHING

In order to hunt and capture the fish and other small sea life that makes up its diet, a seal must be able to stay underwater for a relatively long period of time. The elephant seal can dive and then go without breathing again for at least 20 minutes and perhaps as long as 40 minutes. A trained diver can stay underwater for about two minutes and the average person can seldom hold his breath for more than a minute. It is obvious that the elephant seal has a remarkable breathing system.

There are a number of interrelated actions that take place within the seal's body that make its deep and extended dives possible. For one thing, the elephant seal has about one-and-a-half times more blood in proportion to its size than a human being. This blood is rich in oxygen when the seal begins its dive. This is sufficient to sustain all the necessary body functions during the time it is underwater.

When a seal dives, the air in the lungs is exhaled. This gives it the neutral buoyancy necessary for moving about underwater with the least exertion. The nostrils also close, excluding water from the breathing passages. At the same time, the heartbeat slows down. On the surface, the seal's heart beats about 150 times a minute. During a dive, it beats only 10 or 15 times a minute. Once underwater, all the arteries in the body except those between the heart and the brain are closed down. This is extremely important since this is the way these two vital organs are kept supplied with the oxygen that is necessary for their operation. The rest of the body uses up the oxygen that was present in the tissues and then continues to function without a fresh supply of oxygen until the seal returns to the surface.

Elephant seals flip damp sand onto their backs to help them remain comfortably cool even when the air is quite warm.

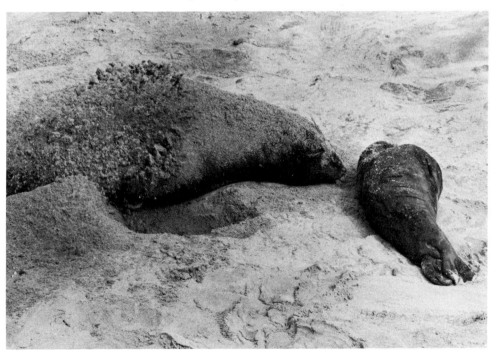

When the seal returns to the surface, its body has what is called an "oxygen debt." This means that its body needs oxygen to replace that which has been used up. After a long dive the seal's body is in somewhat the same condition as a human being that has been exercising hard and is out of breath. Like a human being, the seal "pants" for air. Then, when its oxygen balance is restored, it is ready for another dive.

This specialized breathing does not require any effort on the seal's part. It is completely natural to a seal. So natural that a seal is able to sleep underwater, simply coming to the surface to breathe every few minutes and then sinking back below the surface without waking up.

This is the way the seal has overcome the problem of being an air-breathing mammal that makes its home in the sea. The nostrils, the lungs, the heart, the muscles and indeed the seal's whole body have made special adaptations to make it possible.

BODY HEAT

Because it is warm-blooded, there are many special adaptations that have been made in the seal's body to allow it to function efficiently in surroundings that are constantly colder than its body temperature. As in its specialized breathing, several things work together to make this possible.

First, there is the layer of fat that acts as an insulating blanket over the seal's body, leaving only the flippers uncovered by protective fat. This blubber is very efficient in retaining the seal's body heat. While the skin that is in contact with the water may be just a degree or two above the temperature of the water, the body temperature will be normal, about 99 degrees, only an inch or two into the fat.

Because the seal must live in temperatures that may vary from quite cold to very warm, its body is also capable of making special provisions for this. The blood vessels in a seal's skin, for example, enable his entire body surface to act as a heat exchanger. When the skin is cold, the blood vessels contract so almost no blood is circulated through the skin. In this way very little body

The elephant seal is also uniquely equipped to stay warm since it spends much of its life in cold water.

heat is drained off into the cold water or air around him. But when the seal's skin is warm, the blood vessels expand and blood is pumped through them. Excess body heat is then transferred into the surrounding air or water and the seal is kept cooler. The human body is able to do this, too (the skin is pale when cold, flushed when hot), but only to a much smaller and less efficient degree.

The seal's flippers also aid in controlling the body's temperature. Because the flippers are not protected by fat, it might be thought that much of the blood's heat would be lost through these uninsulated areas. But these too have made special adaptations. The veins carrying the blood back toward the heart run very close alongside the arteries bringing fresh blood from the heart. Most of the heat from the warm blood coming from the heart is transferred to the cooler blood returning from the flippers and in this way no significant amount of heat is lost.

Elephant seals also have another cooling device and this is an external one. It is their "sand flipping" in which they toss sand up onto their backs. The damp sand on the back helps to draw heat away from the skin and this helps to keep the body at a comfortable temperature.

All in all, the seal is a remarkable animal. Every one of its physical characteristics from the streamlined shape of its body to its complicated cooling system is an example of the intricate adaptations it has been able to make in order to survive.

The elephant seals seek out quiet, isolated coves and come
ashore to live for about three months.

Chapter 6
THE SEASON OF SURVIVAL

Just as the seal's body is adapted to its environment, the life cycle of the seal illustrates other ways in which this species is specialized for survival.

The two essential life functions that the elephant seal carries out on land are breeding and giving birth to the young. With the elephant seal, the breeding season takes place within a few weeks after the pupping season. In this way, it is possible to perform these essential activities at the one period of the year when the animals live exclusively on land.

This period of the year, known as the elephant seal's "season," take place during that time of the year that is most favorable for the survival of the young. As the northern elephant seal

In early winter, northern elephant seals gather on remote beaches such as this one at Guadalupe Island.

56

After the cows arrive and select their harems, battles for dominance among the bulls become even more intense.

lives in what we would call a "hot" climate, the pups are born during the milder weather of winter.

The season for the elephant seal begins with the arrival of the mature bulls at the traditional breeding grounds in late November and early December. They congregate on remote islands away from civilization, seeking out isolated coves and beaches.

Upon their arrival the mature bulls stake out their territory, picking a place where it is likely the cows will come ashore. The bulls then defend this space against other bulls. In a small area, the successful bull will drive his rivals away completely. If the area is too large for a single bull to control the entire territory, he simply keeps the others away from the best location.

The cows and the younger animals begin to arrive shortly after this. In a small cove, perhaps as few as six or eight cows will come ashore to join the bull that waits there. Where there is more space, larger groups will congregate. Where there are large areas, such as at Guadalupe Island, there may be several hundred in one group. An area where seals breed and have their young is called a "rookery." The smaller groups of seals are called "harems."

PUPPING

An elephant seal cow gives birth to a pup only once a year and this takes place, usually, within a few days of her arrival. When the cow is ready to give birth, she separates herself from the closely packed group, moving a few feet away. Twin pups are sometimes born but this seems to occur even more rarely than in human beings.

At birth the baby elephant seal is a pitiful looking little black bag of bones with virtually no fat under its skin. Just after it is born, the mother elephant seal spends several minutes sniffing it and nuzzling its body. At this time the mother and baby make noises to each other. It is by this process that the mother and baby become familiar with each other's scent and learn to recognize each other's voices.

Twin pups are sometimes found but this seems to occur even less often than among human beings.

At birth the elephant seal pup is skinny and helpless looking but rapidly puts on weight and gains strength.

Although the new-born pup seems tiny, it is actually about three feet long and weighs about 75 pounds. Its first instinct after birth is that of hunger and it soon finds one of the mother's two teats. The milk of the elephant seal is extremely rich, far richer than the milk of a dairy cow, and the pup puts on weight rapidly with this nutritious diet.

Even during the time when the pup is wholly dependent on the mother for nourishment there is almost nothing that could be called "mother love" displayed by the cow. She allows the baby to nurse but seems to have no other concern for its welfare. She does nothing to protect it from the dangers of harem life, she doesn't teach it to swim or hunt and she doesn't attempt to comfort it when it is hurt.

After the pup is weaned, which is seldom longer than a month after its birth, the pup leaves the mother. From that time on, the cow and pup have nothing more to do with each other. By this point the pup has built up a layer of thick fat under its skin and weighs around 250 pounds. This fat enables it to survive until it is able to get its own food from the sea.

The indifference of the mother seal for her baby is unusual among mammals. In most mammals there are strong bonds of affection between mother and baby. The typical mammal mother protects the baby from harm and shows genuine concern for its welfare. But not the elephant seal mother. Some of the reasons for this will become apparent as we go on with the description of the elephant seal's season.

MOLTING

After the pup leaves the mother, it usually goes further inshore away from the almost continual disturbances common in the harem at this period. Here it will spend most of its time in company with one or two other pups and undergo its first molt. The molting period is a difficult one for all seals and during this time it will spend most of its time sleeping.

Shortly after the pup is born, the mother and baby nuzzle and make noises to each other to become acquainted.

The elephant seal cow's milk is extremely rich and the pup more than doubles its weight in its first month.

During the later stages of the molt when the new, coarse brown hair has replaced the thick, dark gray baby fur, the pup begins to make regular trips into the surf. Now it is developing its coordination and swimming ability. At the age of about four months it is ready to go to sea. By this time the teeth have developed, and its swimming and hunting skills are sufficient to sustain it in the ocean. In its first year it will probably not stay at sea all the time but return to land quite often to rest and sleep. It continues to grow rapidly and by the time it is a year old it will be about six feet long.

BREEDING

For the adult elephant seal, the weaning of the pups heralds the intense activity of the breeding period. The bulls become even more aggressive and there are frequent fights among them to determine which is going to control the preferred territory in the harem.

An encounter between two bulls is an elemental struggle. When they have completed the ritual of the challenge, rearing up and making their distinctive grunting cry, there may or may not be a fight. If one bull decides not to fight, he can usually avoid combat by lying down and remaining silent. The other bull will then ignore him. But if the other bull continues in the challenge position, the fight proceeds.

Unlike some other mammals that fight for domination at breeding time, the object of the battle between elephant seal bulls is domination rather than destruction. That is, these fights are rarely, if ever, carried on until one of the combatants is killed or even seriously injured. Instead, one or the other almost always backs away after only a few blows have been struck.

This dominance of the strongest bulls in the harem is another example of the selective breeding or the "survival of the fittest" that can be observed among most wild animals. The strongest bulls, because they dominate the harem, will mate with the great-

The elephant seal mother allows her pup to nurse but otherwise spends little time caring for it.

During the molting period, the pup is not very active. This one was also inflicted with seal pox at the same time.

est number of cows. Thus the offspring, coming from the strongest stock, will be more likely to survive than if the weaker bulls were allowed to mate freely.

After this season's pup has been weaned, the cow is ready to breed again. A cow mates several times during the breeding period and usually, but not always, with the beachmaster bull. In this way there is the maximum opportunity for the cow to be impregnated and thus assure the arrival of a new pup the next season.

It should now be clear why there is so little display of "mother love" between the elephant seal mother and her baby. During this one season of the year when the cow is ashore, she is extremely busy. Upon arrival at the rookery, she must select her harem. Then she must give birth to this season's pup and nurse it until it is able to survive on its own. After that she immediately enters the breeding period to assure that another pup is born the next season to continue the species. There is simply not time in her schedule for her to guide her pup through a prolonged period of adolescence. And the pup, even without this, is able to survive.

The object of the fight between elephant seal bulls is dominance of the harem rather than to kill the opponent.

DELAYED IMPLANTATION

After the cow has been fertilized by the bull, the fertilized egg develops into a hollow ball of cells and then, for a period of time, the growth of the cells stops. This process is known as delayed implantation and the hollow ball of cells, called a "blastocyst," will not resume its growth until the female has completed her annual molt.

This delayed implantation, which is common to most species of seals, is another of the special adaptations that seals have made to assure the survival of the species. In this way, the female can undergo the difficult molting period without having to provide nourishment for the embryo inside her.

In addition, normal pregnancy resumes in all the fertilized cows at very nearly the same time. It is not known what triggers the embryo to resume its growth in all the cows at almost exactly the same time but there is no doubt that it does occur. By this means, all the pups are born within a relatively short period of

As soon as the pup has been weaned, the elephant seal mother has nothing more to do with the youngster.

Elephant seal cows in the harem are quarrelsome, often having short, noisy spats with their neighbors.

time at the beginning of the next season ashore. It also assures that the next season's pups will be born at that time of the year when the climate is most favorable for their survival.

The elephant seal bull is also controlled by an annual cycle and is physically incapable of mating except at this one season of the year. This is also essential to the continuation of the species. If the males and females were able to mate at periodic intervals throughout the year, as are most mammals, then the pups would be born at random times during the year. If this happened, the newborn pups would have less chance of withstanding the rigors of the climate.

There is little wonder, then, that the season of the elephant seal is one of such intense activity. In one relatively short period the new crop of pups must be born, given their start into an independent adolescence and the breeding rituals carried out that will assure the arrival of a new crop of pups the next season.

We hesitate to say that the seal's life represents a miracle of specialization. There are too many "miracles" in nature to regard the life of one animal as more special than another. But it is apparent that seals have indeed developed remarkable characteristics, both physically and in their life cycle, to assure that they continue to survive.

Chapter 7
THE ONLY ENEMY

The pupping-nursing-breeding period comes to an end for the northern elephant seal in March and early April. The cows begin to return to the sea after breeding and the harems break up.

The next phase of the annual cycle of the elephant seal is the annual molt. The seal goes to sea, feeds intensively to build up the reserves of fat that were used up during its stay on land, then returns to land again to molt. Most species of seals simply lose their old hair at this time but the elephant seal also loses large patches of skin at the same time. It takes about a month for the new coat to grow. After this it returns to the ocean again, this time to stay until the pupping period arrives.

Little is known about the habits of elephant seals when they

It is likely that most elephant seals die of natural causes when they become too old to continue hunting.

Mature elephant seal bull, his hide marked with the scars of many battles, will live to be about 20 years old.

Young bull whose snout is just developing. He will be about 14 years old before participating in harem life.

are at sea. It is known, however, that they are solitary animals. That is, unlike whales and porpoises, they do not travel in herds or packs when they are in the ocean. This characteristic is apparently reserved for the season when they are on land.

The female elephant seal is capable of bearing young at about the age of four or five. The cow then has a pup every year until about the age of 12.

The male elephant seal becomes sexually mature at about six years of age. But because the young bull is not sufficiently strong to hold a place in the harem until it is at least 14 years old, a bull is rarely able to breed before that age. The elephant seal bull lives to be about 20 years old.

The elephant seal has almost no natural enemies, either on land or in the water. On land, for example, man is the elephant seal's only enemy. Even a pack of dogs, which will attack and kill an animal as large and vicious as a bear, will avoid contact with elephant seals. In the water it has been speculated that killer whales and large sharks will attack an elephant seal. The only evidence that has been presented to confirm this results from elephant seals that have been found with scars on their bodies that suggest they may have been attacked by these predators when they were quite small.

It is likely that most elephant seal adults live to a ripe old elephant seal age and then die of natural causes. Weakened by parasites, their teeth worn down by years of use, their eyesight dimmed with age, they become less efficient hunters and are unable to capture sufficient food to sustain life.

Up to the present time there is no evidence that oil spills, DDT or other pollutants dumped into the oceans by man have had any effect on the elephant seal. The continuing pollution of the oceans is a cause for concern, however. Now that we have become aware of the problem, careful observation by biologists should help to prevent any such damage in the future.

For all the remarkable specialization made by the elephant

Remains of some of the equipment used by the seal hunters many years ago on Guadalupe Island, Baja California.

Although now protected by law, permission has been given for a few elephant seals to be captured for study.

seal for its survival, it was not equipped to resist its only enemy, man.

Because they had no natural enemies on land, the elephant seals were not alarmed when men arrived on their islands during the early 1800s. It therefore took neither skill nor courage to kill great numbers of them for their oil.

Considering the greed of the seal hunters, we are extremely fortunate that there are any northern elephant seals left at all. After they began to be hunted in the early 1800s, they were killed in such great numbers that by 1885 they were thought to be extinct.

In 1907 a group that numbered less than a hundred were discovered on a rocky, desolate coast of Guadalupe Island. It is believed that this small number were all the northern elephant seals that had escaped the hunters.

Because this tiny band of survivors was too small to be of commercial value for their oil, the Meixcan government met no resistance when it imposed restrictions on further killing in 1911. In 1922 they were given absolute protection and since that time northern elephant seals have not been killed for commercial purposes. In recent years, now that the species is in no immediate danger of disappearing, permission has been granted for a few to be taken for study by scientists and for others to be captured for display in zoos and marine exhibits.

As the northern elephant seal population continues to grow, it is possible that pressure may be brought on the U.S. and Mexican governments to allow the "surplus" population to be "harvested." This is already being done with southern elephant seals in the antarctic. There it is strictly controlled and represents a valuable contribution to the economy of the people who live in that remote area.

Something similar may be advocated for the northern elephant seal but with the present attitude most people have about wildlife, this may be avoided.

The bull elephant seal's snout is long and hollow. It is used as an echo chamber for his distinctive grunt.

Epilogue

While it may seem remarkable that any mammal could have made such a large number of specialized adaptations for survival, those made by the seal are no more miraculous than those of many other animals. Every animal that exists is specialized for survival in many ways.

The examples are everywhere around us. The beaver's tail is not only useful for swimming but in his building projects as well. The long neck of the giraffe almost certainly developed to allow it to feed on vegetation that was too high off the ground for other animals to reach. Through necessity, the camel developed the ability to go without water for days and weeks at a time. Even more specialized, in the desert there is the tiny kangaroo mouse that does not drink water during its entire life!

Nor is such specialization restricted to the world of mammals. Birds are equally good examples. The beak of the meat-eating bird is efficiently curved for ripping its food while the seed-eater's beak is stubby and strong for cracking shells. The hummingbird's long beak is exactly right for sipping nectar from deep, bell-shaped flowers.

By studying the animals, it is possible to discover the reasons for the special characteristics they possess that make them different from other animals. Why does the elephant have a trunk? Is it because its mouth is awkwardly located for grazing and something like the trunk has developed to bring food to its mouth?

Specialized adaptations can be detected in even the most common animals. Everyone knows that the eyes of a cat enable it to see in very dim light. Was this not a specialization to make it an efficient hunter of the small, nocturnal rodents that are its natural food?

And why are a cat's teeth pointed and sharp while those of a cow are flat and broad? Is it not because a cat is a hunter that must kill its prey while the cow, a vegetarian, needs teeth that are efficient in chewing its food?

It can be fascinating to puzzle over these things, trying to find the reasons for the specialized characteristics of different animals. It is even more fascinating because there sometimes seems to be

75

The bull's snout seems to be more of a bother than a useful
appendage. Can you guess why it was developed?

no answer even for the most obvious characteristics. The snout of the elephant seal bull, for instance. Why has it developed? What is its purpose? Has it no other function than to act as an echo chamber for its grunting battle cry? No one has ever figured that out.

Can you?

Bibliography

OTHER BOOKS ABOUT SEALS

K. M. Backhouse, *Seals*, Golden Press, New York, 1969

Ewan Clarkson, *Halic, the Story of a Gray Seal*, E. P. Dutton & Co., New York, 1970

Gary Gaetz, *Rookery Island*, Rand McNally & Co., New York, 1967

Nina Warner Hooke, *The Seal Summer*, Harcourt Brace & World, New York, 1964

Fredericka Martin, *Sea Bears, the Story of the Fur Seal*, Chilton Co., Philadelphia and New York, 1960.

L. Harrison Matthews, *Sea Elephant*, Macgibbon & Kee, London, 1952

Gavin Maxwell, *Seals of the World*, Houghton Mifflin Co., Boston, 1967

R. H. Pearson, *A Seal Flies By*, Hart-Davis, London, 1959

Charles M. Scammon, *The Marine Mammals of the Northwestern Coast of North America*, Dover, New York, 1968, (originally published in 1874)

Victor B. Scheffer, *The Year of the Seal*, Chas Scribner's Sons, New York, 1970

Victor B. Scheffer, *Seals, Sea Lions & Walruses*, Stanford University, 1958

Frank Stuart, *A Seal's World*, George C. Harrap & Co., London, 1954

ABOUT THE AUTHOR

As the editor of *Road & Track* magazine since 1965, James T. Crow has written innumerable articles (as well as three books) on automotive subjects. It was his special interest in travel and western history that led him to the San Benito Islands in Mexico to observe, first-hand, an elephant seal colony. Mr. Crow's first questions, "How does a seal operate? How does a seal work?" in turn led to the months of research that resulted in *SURVIVAL OF A SPECIES: The Elephant Seal.* Mr. Crow says, "For anyone who is interested in observing animals and attempting to understand them, the elephant seal is a remarkable and rewarding study."

ABOUT THE PHOTOGRAPHER

Gordon E. Chittenden admits to many adventures during his career as a free lance photographer. His previously published works include "How To Photograph Auto Racing", as well as assignments from major magazines all over the world. However, the "thrill" of being charged by a bull elephant seal, while photographing the seal colony on the remote San Benito Islands for this book, is one of the few times a near-miss has been recorded on film (see page 27.)